# 5th Grade

# ALABAMA

# ELA
# TEST
# PREP

# Common Core
# State Standards

# INTRODUCTION

Our 5th Grade ELA Test Prep for Common Core State Standards is an excellent resource to supplement your classroom's curriculum to assess and manage students' understanding of concepts outlined in the Common Core State Standards Initiative for Reading Literature and Reading Informational Text. There are several questions aligned to each Common Core Standard Reading Literature and Informational Text standard. We recommend the student read the story passage and answer the questions that follow each story in the book. The answers marked by the student can serve as a diagnostic tool to determine WHY the student had an incorrect answer. The answer to the student's misunderstanding is NOT another worksheet, but a re-teaching of the skill, using different instructional strategies.

The reason for incorrect answers is often the result of the student using an incorrect procedure. Most of the errors we see as teachers and parents are the same each year. Students apply a rule in an inappropriate way. Many times they will even say to us, "That's what you said to do." They see logic in the way they have applied the rule even though it is incorrect. Therefore, it is imperative to determine WHY a student chose an incorrect answer to a question. The best way to determine this is to ask the student to explain their reasoning to you.

All questions in this product are aligned to the current Common Core State Standards Initiative. To view the standards, refer to pages *i* through *ii*.

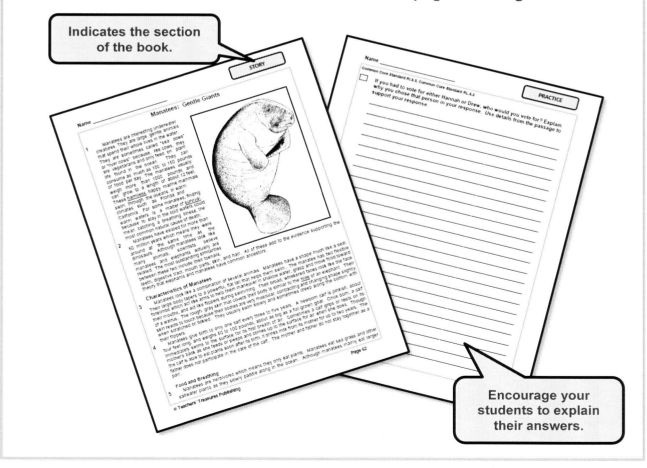

Indicates the section of the book.

Encourage your students to explain their answers.

# 5th Grade
# ELA Test Prep
## FOR
# Common Core Standards

## COMMON CORE STATE STANDARDS

| Reading Literature - Key Ideas and Details | RL.5.1 |
|---|---|

Quote accurately from a text when explaining what the text says explicitly and when drawing inferences from the text.

| Reading Literature – Key Ideas and Details | RL.5.2 |
|---|---|

Determine a theme of a story, drama, or poem from details in the text, including how characters in a story or drama respond to challenges or how the speaker in a poem reflects upon a topic; summarize the text.

| Reading Literature – Key Ideas and Details | RL.5.3 |
|---|---|

Compare and contrast two or more characters, settings, or events in a story or drama, drawing on specific details in the text (e.g., how characters interact).

| Reading Literature – Craft and Structure | RL.5.4 |
|---|---|

Determine the meaning of words and phrases as they are used in a text, including figurative language such as metaphors and similes.

| Reading Literature – Craft and Structure | RL.5.5 |
|---|---|

Explain how a series of chapters, scenes, or stanzas fits together to provide the overall structure of a particular story, drama, or poem.

| Reading Literature – Craft and Structure | RL.5.6 |
|---|---|

Describe how a narrator's or speaker's point of view influences how events are described.

| Reading Literature – Integration of Knowledge and Ideas | RL.5.7 |
|---|---|

Analyze how visual and multimedia elements contribute to the meaning, tone, or beauty of a text (e.g., graphic novel, multimedia presentation of fiction, folktale, myth, poem).

| Reading Literature – Integration of Knowledge and Ideas | RL.5.8 |
|---|---|

(RL.5.8 not applicable to literature)

| Reading Literature – Integration of Knowledge and Ideas | RL.5.9 |
|---|---|

Compare and contrast stories in the same genre (e.g., mysteries and adventure stories) on their approaches to similar themes and topics.

| Reading Literature – Range of Reading and Level of Text Complexity | RL.5.10 |
|---|---|

By the end of the year, read and comprehend literature, including stories, dramas, and poetry, at the high end of the grades 4–5 text complexity band independently and proficiently.

**Reading Informational Text – Key Ideas and Details**     RI.5.1

Quote accurately from a text when explaining what the text says explicitly and when drawing inferences from the text.

**Reading Informational Text – Key Ideas and Details**     RI.5.2

Determine a theme of a story, drama, or poem from details in the text, including how characters in a story or drama respond to challenges or how the speaker in a poem reflects upon a topic; summarize the text.

**Reading Informational Text – Key Ideas and Details**     RI.5.3

Compare and contrast two or more characters, settings, or events in a story or drama, drawing on specific details in the text (e.g., how characters interact).

**Reading Informational Text – Craft and Structure**     RI.5.4

Determine the meaning of words and phrases as they are used in a text, including figurative language such as metaphors and similes.

**Reading Informational Text – Craft and Structure**     RI.5.5

Explain how a series of chapters, scenes, or stanzas fits together to provide the overall structure of a particular story, drama, or poem.

**Reading Informational Text – Craft and Structure**     RI.5.6

Describe how a narrator's or speaker's point of view influences how events are described.

**Reading Informational Text – Integration of Knowledge and Ideas**     RI.5.7

Analyze how visual and multimedia elements contribute to the meaning, tone, or beauty of a text (e.g., graphic novel, multimedia presentation of fiction, folktale, myth, poem).

**Reading Informational Text – Integration of Knowledge and Ideas**     RI.5.8

(RL.5.8 not applicable to literature)

**Reading Informational Text – Integration of Knowledge and Ideas**     RI.5.9

Compare and contrast stories in the same genre (e.g., mysteries and adventure stories) on their approaches to similar themes and topics.

**Reading Informational Text – Range of Reading and Level of Text Complexity**     RI.5.10

By the end of the year, read and comprehend literature, including stories, dramas, and poetry, at the high end of the grades 4–5 text complexity band independently and proficiently.

# What is celebrated on *Dia de los Muertos*?

*El Dia de lost Muertos*, or All Souls' Day as it is called in English, is an <u>ancient</u> festivity that has been changed through the years, but which was intended to celebrate children and the dead. Sometimes this day is also called "The Day of the Dead." This Mexican holiday is a time when Mexican families remember their dead family members and the <u>continuing</u> of life.

## How It Began

Many years ago the festivities were part of the Aztec Indian culture. Their celebration occurred at the end of July and the beginning of August.

The Day of the Dead now begins on October 31st and is celebrated during the first two days of November. The activities begin with the families visiting the graves of their dead relatives. The family members clean the gravesite and decorate it with large, bright flowers such as chrysanthemums and marigolds. The families and community members that gather at the cemetery have a picnic where they <u>relate</u> stories about their dead family members. The delicious meals prepared for these picnics include meat dishes in <u>spicy</u> sauces, a special egg-battered bread, and cookies, chocolate, and sugary confections in a variety of animal or skull shapes.

## Altar Decorations

Mexican families build special home altars dedicated to the spirits of their <u>deceased</u> loved ones. Some altars are simple while others are very <u>elaborate</u>. An altar usually begins with a table on which boxes are placed to represent the tombs. All of it is covered with a white tablecloth or sheet. Long <u>stalks</u> of sugarcane are tied to the front legs of the table and form a triangular arc above the altar. Flowers, candles, photos, and objects, such as

favorite foods, that provided pleasure to the dead person are placed on the table. Altars <u>dedicated</u> to the spirits of dead children often include toys, candy, and other sweets.

## How the Celebration Has Changed

Long ago the Day of the Dead celebration began in the early morning hours of November the 2nd with a feast. Now most Mexican families have a special family supper where they serve the "Bread of the Dead," *pan de muerto.* It is good luck to the one who bites into the plastic toy skeleton hidden by the baker in each rounded loaf of bread. Friends and family members give each other gifts of sugar skeletons or other items with a death design.

## Visitors to Mexico

During the week of the celebration many tourists visit cities in Mexico. They come to learn about a culture different from their own. They <u>respectfully</u> observe and appreciate all of the festivities. The visitors are welcome to spend time in the cemeteries, and enjoy the beauty of the decorations and the delicious food of the season.

During the celebration stores sell candy skulls and *calaveras* (skeletons) made of wood, paper mache, clay, and wax. The miniature skeletons look like fishermen, doctors, judges, teachers, tennis players, and other occupations. Some of the skeletons can even be life-size. Candy skulls are made by pouring a mixture of boiling water, confectioner's sugar, and lime into clay molds which have been previously soaked in water. Mexican children often exchange named skulls with their friends. Mexican people view the skeletons and skulls as funny and friendly, rather than spooky and scary.

**Common Core Standard RI5.4**

☐    In this passage, the word <u>ancient</u> means _____

A    new

B    undeveloped

C    very old

D    exciting

**Common Core Standard RI.5.4; Common Core Standard RL.5.4**

☐    In this passage, the word <u>relate</u> means _____

A    tell

B    write

C    draw pictures

D    read

**Common Core Standard RI.5.4**

☐    In this passage, the word <u>deceased</u> means _____

A    old

B    departed

C    friendly

D    angry

**Name** _____

Common Core Standard RI.5.4; Common Core Standard RL.5.4

☐  In this passage, the **elaborate** means _____

A  old

B  bright

C  fresh

D  fancy

Common Core Standard RI.5.4; Common Core Standard RL.5.4

☐  In this passage, the word **stalks** means _____

A  to track something or someone

B  slender stems

C  flowers

D  bags

Common Core Standard RI.5.4; Common Core Standard RL.5.4

☐  In this passage, the word **dedicated** means _____

A  made for

B  next to

C  make a hole

D  difficult

**Common Core Standard RI.5.4; Common Core Standard RL54.4**

☐   **In this passage, the word <u>continuing</u> means _____**

   **A**    **to stop**

   **B**    **above**

   **C**    **gone**

   **D**    **ongoing**

**Common Core Standard RI.5.4**

☐   **In this passage, the word <u>spicy</u> means _____**

   **A**    **thin**

   **B**    **well-seasoned**

   **C**    **salty**

   **D**    **thick**

**Common Core Standard RI.5.4**

☐   **In this passage, the word <u>respectfully</u> means _____**

   **A**    **important**

   **B**    **watch**

   **C**    **well-mannered**

   **D**    **unpleasant**

**Common Core Standard RI.5.1; Common Core Standard RI.5.5**

☐   **Which of these events happens first during the Day of the Dead celebration?**

A       The families decorate the gravesite with flowers.

B       The families go to the cemeteries where their relatives are buried.

C       The families have a special family supper.

D       The families build an altar.

---

**Common Core Standard RI.5.4**

☐   **According to the passage, what is the last day of the celebration?**

A       November 3

B       October 31

C       November 1

D       November 2

---

**Common Core Standard RI.5.1; Common Core Standard RI.5.5**

☐   **Which of these do the families do before they have a picnic?**

A       Have a family supper

B       Buy candy skulls

C       Visit the graves of their dead relatives

D       Visit with tourists

---

Common Core Standard RI.5.1

☐    **According to the passage, what will happen to the person who finds the toy skeleton in their piece of bread?**

    **A**     They will hide the toy skeleton next time.

    **B**     They will be responsible for serving the dinner next year.

    **C**     They will have good luck.

    **D**     They will buy skull candy for their family.

Common Core Standard RI.5.1

☐    **How many days does the Day of the Dead celebration last?**

    **A**     Four

    **B**     One

    **C**     Two

    **D**     Three

Common Core Standard RI.5.1

☐    **Why do the families build an altar in their homes?  Use details from the story in your explanation.**

_____

_____

_____

_____

_____

**Name** _____

---

Common Core Standard RI.5.7

☐ **When do most Mexican families serve the special dinner?**

A    November 1

B    November 2

C    November 3

D    October 31

---

Common Core Standard RI.5.7

☐ **Where would most Mexican families be found on November 1st?**

A    Shopping

B    At the special evening meal

C    At the cemetery

D    Baking bread

---

Common Core Standard RI.5.1; Common Core Standard RI.5.7

☐ **According to the passage, where would most Mexican families place photos of the dead family members?**

A    On the altar

B    In the stores

C    At the gravesite

D    On the feast table

---

**Common Core Standard RI.5.2**

☐ **The passage is mostly about _____**

A    toy skulls

B    baking bread

C    building an altar

D    remembering the dead

**Common Core Standard RI.5.2**

☐ **What is the main idea of the section "How It Began?"**

_____

_____

_____

_____

_____

**Common Core Standard RI.5.2**

☐ **What is the main idea of the first paragraph in the section "Visitors to Mexico?"**

_____

_____

_____

_____

_____

Name _____

Common Core Standard RI.5.2; Common Core Standard RL.5.2

☐   **Which is the best summary of this passage?**

A   Tourists can participate in the celebration when they visit Mexico.

B   During the celebration the families eat lots of sweets.

C   The families honor their dead by building altars, eating, visiting the cemetery, and talking about the dead family members during three days in the fall of each year.

D   The altars show favorites of the dead family member.

Common Core Standard RI.5.2; Common Core Standard RL.5.2

☐   **Which of these is the best summary of the section "Altar Decorations?"**

A   Altars are built in homes to help the families remember what the dead family member liked.

B   Altars for dead children may have toys and candy on them.

C   Most of the altars are decorated with flowers.

D   Sugarcane is used to form an arc above the altar.

Common Core Standard RI.5.2; Common Core Standard RL.5.2

☐   **Which of these is the best summary of the section "How the Celebration Has Changed?"**

A   Friends give sugar skeletons to each other.

B   The celebration began early in the morning long ago.

C   Bread is served at the dinner.

D   A family supper is held on November 2nd where special bread is served.

Common Core Standard RI.5.5

☐  Flowers, candles, and photos are placed on the altars because _____

A     the families are planning a special meal

B     the Aztec Indians built altars

C     family members give sugar skeletons as gifts

D     the families want to honor the dead family member

Common Core Standard RI.5.5

☐  The Mexican families visit the cemeteries because _____

A     they are sad

B     they need to clean the gravesite

C     they want to have a picnic

D     they bought some flowers

Common Core Standard RI.5.5

☐  Most Mexican families serve "Bread of the Dead" because _____

A     it tastes good

B     the bakeries have it for sale

C     it is an important part of the celebration

D     it is made of egg-batter

Name _____

Common Core Standard RI.5.5; Common Core Standard RL.5.5

☐ **Mexican families use skulls and skeletons in their decorations because they ____**

A    are sad

B    are not afraid of them

C    can be bought at the stores

D    exchange them with their friends

Common Core Standard RI.5.5; Common Core Standard RL.5.5

☐ **Why do Mexican families decorate the gravesite and altar with flowers?**

A    The flowers are easy to find.

B    They like yellow flowers.

C    They want them to be attractive.

D    The Aztec Indians used flowers many years ago.

Common Core Standard RI.5.5; Common Core Standard RL.5.5

☐ **Why do people visit Mexico during the celebration?**

A    The Day of the Dead is an unusual celebration.

B    They like to eat sweets.

C    They want to work in the cemeteries.

D    They will help build the altars.

**Name** _____

---

Common Core Standard RI.5.8

☐ Based on the information in the passage, the reader can conclude that _____

A    many of the activities were once done by the Aztec Indians

B    this celebration has been held for 100 years

C    Mexican families do not care about their dead relatives

D    the stores make a lot of money during the celebration

---

Common Core Standard RI.5.8; Common Core Standard RL.5.1

☐ According to the passage, what part of the celebration has changed over the years?

A    The picnic is held on November 1st.

B    Mexican children exchange skulls with their friends.

C    The Day of the Dead is held in the fall instead of the summer.

D    Miniature skeletons are made to look like doctors, judges, and teachers.

---

Common Core Standard RI.5.8; Common Core Standard RL.5.1

☐ Today the purpose of the Day of the Dead is to _____

A    have a party

B    sell items in the stores

C    entertain the tourists

D    celebrate life

---

Common Core Standard RI.5.9, Common Core Standard RL.5.9

☐    According to the passage, most of the activities of the Day of the Dead are designed to make _____

A    the families sad

B    money for the store owners

C    Mexican families remember the good times with their relatives

D    the families prepare food for the celebration

Common Core Standard RI.5.9, Common Core Standard RL.5.9

☐    According to the passage, what is NOT an important part of the festivities?

A    Food

B    Souvenirs

C    Flowers

D    Dancing

Common Core Standard RI.5.9, Common Core Standard RL.5.9

☐    Many of the cookies and candies are formed into the shape of skulls because _____

A    they are easy to make

B    the festivities are about the dead

C    tourists like to buy them

D    they are scary

Common Core Standard RI.5.8, Common Core Standard RL.5.3

☐ **How do the tourists probably feel when they visit Mexico during the Day of the Dead festivities?**

A    Angry

B    Curious

C    Frightened

D    Uninterested

---

Common Core Standard RI.5.8, Common Core Standard RL.5.3

☐ **How do the Mexican families probably feel during the Day of the Dead?**

A    Sad and angry

B    Upset and scared

C    Happy and sad

D    Anxious and happy

---

Common Core Standard RI.5.8, Common Core Standard RL.5.3

☐ **The passage gives you reason to believe that the Mexican families _____**

A    spend a lot of money during the celebration

B    are frightened by all of the skeletons and skulls

C    want their celebration different from the Aztec festival

D    look forward to the festivities

**Common Core Standard RL.5.2**

☐ **The reader can tell that _____**

    **A**    this celebration is different from most American celebrations

    **B**    most people dread the festivities

    **C**    the children are frightened by the visit to the cemetery

    **D**    this is not an important Mexican holiday

**Common Core Standard RL.5.2**

☐ **The passage suggests that _____**

    **A**    the festivities are not interesting

    **B**    tourists tease the Mexican families

    **C**    marigolds are the only flowers used for decorating

    **D**    the Day of the Dead is a very old festival

**Common Core Standard RL.5.2**

☐ **Based on information in the passage, the Mexican families are _____**

    **A**    afraid of the tourists

    **B**    not frightened when visiting the cemetery

    **C**    tired of the celebration

    **D**    hoping they do not find the toy skeleton in their bread

Common Core Standard RL.5.6

☐ **Which is a FACT in this passage?**

A    Many people from America visit Mexico during the Day of the Dead.

B    The children collect the different kinds of skull candy.

C    An egg-batter bread is a special food served at the picnic.

D    Mexican families invite their relatives to visit the week of the festivities.

---

Common Core Standard RL.5.6

☐ **Which is a FACT in this passage?**

A    Candy skulls are made from sugar and water.

B    People dress up in costumes during the celebration.

C    The home altar is set up in the dining room.

D    The spicy meat dishes at the picnic are made of beef and ham.

---

Common Core Standard RL.5.6

☐ **Which is an OPINION in this passage?**

A    Another name for the celebration is All Souls' Day.

B    Some of the skeletons are life-size.

C    Many of the souvenirs have a death design on them.

D    After the families clean the gravesite, decorate it, and have a picnic, they are very tired.

Name _____

---

Common Core Standard RI.5.8

☐   The author probably wrote this passage in order to _____

A     inform the reader about a Mexican holiday

B     persuade the reader to visit Mexico

C     describe the Aztec Indians

D     explain how skull candy is made

---

Common Core Standard RI.5.8

☐   An article like this one could be found in _____

A     a cookbook

B     a novel

C     a comic book

D     a travel magazine

---

Common Core Standard RI.5.8

☐   A student could use information from this passage to _____

A     scare his friends

B     plan a trip to Europe

C     write a story about Mexican holidays

D     influence her teacher

---

Common Core Standard RI.5.3, Common Core Standard RL.5.6

☐ **The author of this passage probably _____**

A    is superstitious

B    is afraid of skeletons

C    has been to a Day of the Dead celebration

D    is an American

Common Core Standard RI.5.3, Common Core Standard RL.5.6

☐ **The author of this passage probably likes to _____**

A    eat

B    read

C    ride trains

D    attend festivals

Common Core Standard RI.5.3, Common Core Standard RL.5.6

☐ **How do you know the author of this passage can probably speak Spanish?**

A    The article is about a Mexican holiday.

B    There are Spanish words in the passage.

C    The Day of the Dead takes place in Mexico.

D    The passage tells about Mexican food.

Common Core Standard RI.5.3, Common Core Standard RL.5.6

☐ **The author of this passage wrote about the *Dia de los Muertos* festival. How would you describe the festival to someone who had never heard of *Dia de los Muertos*? Use details from the passage to support your response.**

_____

_____

_____

_____

_____

_____

_____

_____

_____

_____

_____

_____

_____

_____

_____

_____

_____

_____

_____

_____

_____

_____

_____

# Who will win the essay contest?

1    Jeremy, Ontario, and Louisa were enjoying chocolate sundaes at Izzy's Ice Cream Parlor when they noticed a poster advertising an <u>upcoming</u> Father's Day Essay Contest.  Since they like to write stories and poetry, they knew this was something they had a good chance of winning.

2    The next day at school they told their teacher, Mr. Washburn, about the contest.  Mr. Washburn thought it would be an interesting assignment for all of his students.  However, before the students wrote their essays, Mr. Washburn wanted the students to learn about the origin of Father's Day.  When he asked the students how Father's Day came into being, none of the students had an answer.

3    Mr. Washburn provided the following article for the students to read.

---

### Father's Day History

4    Father's Day is celebrated on the third Sunday in June. The idea for creating a day for children to honor their fathers began in Spokane, Washington. A woman by the name of Sonora Smart Dodd thought of the idea for Father's Day while listening to a Mother's Day sermon at church in 1909.

5    Sonora wanted a special day to honor her father who was a Civil War <u>veteran</u>. Sonora had been raised by her father on a <u>rural</u> farm in eastern Washington state after her mother had died.  There were six children, including Sonora in her family.  She wanted her father to know how special he was to her.  It was her father that made all the parental  sacrifices and was, in her eyes, a courageous, <u>selfless</u>, and  loving man.  Because her father celebrated his birthday in June, she chose to hold the first Father's Day celebration in Spokane on June 19, 1910.

6    Even before Sonora Dodd, the idea of observing a day in honor of fathers was promoted. Dr. Robert Webb conducted what is believed to be the first Father's Day service at the Central Church of Fairmont, West Virginia, in 1908. It was Sonora's efforts, however, that eventually led to a national observance.

7    In 1924 President Calvin Coolidge proclaimed the third Sunday in June as Father's Day.  In 1966 President Lyndon Johnson signed a presidential proclamation declaring the third Sunday of June as Father's Day.

8    Roses are the Father's Day flower.  Red roses are to be worn for a living father and white if the father has died.

---

9    Mr. Washburn went to the ice cream parlor and told Izzy, the owner, about the students' assignment.  Izzy gave Mr. Washburn one of the posters that he had displayed on the windows so the students could follow the rules of the contest.  When Mr. Washburn showed the students the poster, they were <u>thrilled</u> about the <u>challenge</u> the contest provided.

# Izzy's Ice Cream Parlor's Annual Father's Day Essay Contest

**Deadline for all entries is June 1**

**Is your dad really special? Does he deserve to be "The Father of the Year?" This contest is the perfect opportunity for you to tell all the world why your dad is so wonderful!**

1. All entrants must be between the ages of 7 and 15.
2. Three winners will be selected in each of the following categories: 7-9; 10-12; 13-15.
3. Essays must be original work and must be at least 100 words, but no longer than 300 words.
4. All essays must be typed and double-spaced.
5. Please include a recent photo of you with your dad.
6. Your essay should focus on what makes your dad deserve the title, "Father of the Year."
7. Essays will be judged on:
   a. creativity
   b. <u>elaboration</u>
   c. punctuation
   d. spelling
8. Winners will be announced June 3rd. Winners will receive the following prizes:
   1st prize - $100 plus $150 gift certificate to Izzy's
   2nd prize - $50 plus $100 gift certificate to Izzy's
   3rd prize - $25 plus $50 gift certificate to Izzy's
9. Pictures of all essay winners and their dads, as well as their essays, will appear in *The Local News* on Father's Day, June 11th!

The entry form below must be attached to all entries.

| | |
|---|---|
| Name_____ | Age_____ |
| Father's Name_____ | |
| Signature_____ | |

**Essays and pictures become the <u>property</u> of Izzy's Ice Cream Parlor and will not be returned.**

10    "I want to write a really <u>superb</u> essay because my dad is very special!" exclaimed Jeremy. "He is always taking me to baseball games, the batting cages, and pitching with me in the front yard."

11    "Your entry will have to compete against mine," Louisa replied half jokingly. "My dad gets up early on Saturday and makes pancakes for us. He never misses one of my soccer games and, also, goes to college at night after he has worked all day."

12    "That's nothing!" Ontario offered. "My dad teaches school all day and then coaches the basketball team. He also coaches our church basketball team and still has time to help me with my homework.

Common Core Standard RI.5.4; Common Core Standard RL.5.4

☐ **Read the meanings below for the word thrill.**

**Which meaning best fits the way thrilled is used in paragraph 9?**

A    Meaning 3

B    Meaning 1

C    Meaning 4

D    Meaning 2

thrill ('thril) *verb*
1. to have or cause to have a sudden feeling of excitement or pleasure
2. to quiver or cause to quiver
*noun*
3. a trembling
4. something that produces great excitement

---

Common Core Standard RI.5.4; Common Core Standard RL.5.4

☐ **Read the meanings below for the word property.**

**Which meaning best fits the way property is used on the contest poster?**

A    Meaning 2

B    Meaning 3

C    Meaning 1

D    Meaning 4

property ('präp-ert-ē) *noun*
1. a special quality of a thing
2. something that is owned
3. something other than scenery or costumes that is used in a play or movie
4. ownership

---

Common Core Standard RI.5.4; Common Core Standard RL.5.4

☐ **Read the meanings below for the word challenge.**

**Which meaning best fits the way challenge is used in paragraph 9?**

A    Meaning 3

B    Meaning 2

C    Meaning 4

D    Meaning 1

challenge ('chal-enj) *verb*
1. to halt and demand a password from
2. to object to as bad or incorrect
*noun*
3. a demand that someone take part in a duel
4. a call or dare for someone to compete in a contest or sport

Common Core Standard RI.5.4; Common Core Standard RL.5.4

☐     **In paragraph 5, the word <u>veteran</u> means _____**

    **A**     adult male

    **B**     famous person

    **C**     experienced person

    **D**     very old

Common Core Standard RI.5.4; Common Core Standard RL.5.4

☐     **In paragraph 5, the word <u>rural</u> means _____**

    **A**     containing many acres

    **B**     cattle ranch

    **C**     small and isolated

    **D**     not in a city

Common Core Standard RI.5.4; Common Core Standard RL.5.4

☐     **In paragraph 10, the word <u>superb</u> means _____**

    **A**     the winner

    **B**     first-class

    **C**     very long

    **D**     not easy

Common Core Standard RI.5.4; Common Core Standard RL.5.4

☐ **In paragraph 1, the word <u>upcoming</u> means _____**

A     annual

B     very popular

C     approaching

D     extremely difficult

---

Common Core Standard RI.5.4; Common Core Standard RL.5.4

☐ **In paragraph 5, the word <u>selfless</u> means _____**

A     lacking confidence

B     unselfish

C     devoted

D     humble

---

Common Core Standard RI.5.4; Common Core Standard RL.5.4

☐ **In the contest poster, the word <u>elaboration</u> means _____**

A     length

B     use of long phrases

C     lacking errors

D     filled with details

---

Name _____

Common Core Standard RI.5.2

☐ **Paragraph 5 is mainly about _____**

A    Sonora's life as a small girl

B    Sonora's desire to honor her father

C    living on a farm

D    the qualities of a good father

Common Core Standard RI.5.2

☐ **Izzy gave Mr. Washburn a poster because _____**

A    Father's Day is rapidly approaching

B    each student will need to turn in a copy of the poster with their essay

C    the students need to follow the rules of the contest when they write their essays

D    all of the prizes are money and gift certificates

Common Core Standard RI.5.2

☐ **Mr. Washburn gave the students the article about Father's Day to read because _____**

A    none of the students knew how Father's Day had begun

B    it would be an interesting assignment

C    it will soon be Father's Day

D    Mr. Washburn is a father

Name _____

Common Core Standard RL.5.2

☐     **Which is the best summary of <u>Who will win the essay contest</u>?**

A     Mr. Washburn's class read an article about Father's Day.  If they win the contest, each student will receive money and gift certificates.  Ontario thinks he will win.

B     Jeremy, Ontario, and Louisa told Mr. Washburn, their teacher, about an essay contest sponsored by Izzy's Ice Cream Parlor.  Mr. Washburn wants the students to enter the contest.  Father's Day happens every June.

C     When Jeremy, Ontario, and Louisa told Mr. Washburn about an essay contest, he gave the students an article to read about Father's Day.  He told the students that they were to write an essay about their father.  Izzy gave Mr. Washburn a poster for the students to copy.  Jeremy thinks he will win because his dad is special.  Louisa's dad goes to college, and Ontario's dad is a coach.

D     Three of Mr. Washburn's students told him about the Father's Day Essay Contest sponsored by Izzy's Ice Cream Parlor.  Mr. Washburn told the students their assignment was to write an essay about their father.  He gave them an article to read about Father's Day.  Mr. Washburn told Izzy about the students' assignment, so Izzy gave him a poster about the contest.  Each student thinks they will win because they all believe they have the best dad.

Common Core Standard RL.5.3

☐ **What can the reader tell about Sonora Dodd?**

    **A**     She liked her father better than she liked her mother.

    **B**     She was very poor.

    **C**     She believed that fathers as well as mothers should be honored on a special day.

    **D**     She believed that fathers are more important than mothers.

Common Core Standard RL.5.3

☐ **The reader can tell that Izzy wants _____**

    **A**     Mr. Washburn to force the students to enter the contest

    **B**     the students to follow the rules of the contest so that they will have a chance to win

    **C**     the winner of the contest to be a student in Mr. Washburn's class

    **D**     everyone to visit his ice cream parlor

Common Core Standard RL.5.3

☐ **Which of the following best describes Jeremy, Ontario, and Louisa?**

    **A**     Bossy

    **B**     Confident

    **C**     Anxious

    **D**     Competitive

Common Core Standard RI.5.7

☐ **Based on information in the contest poster, what time of the year is it?**

    **A**    Summer

    **B**    Fall

    **C**    Winter

    **D**    Spring

Common Core Standard RI.5.7

☐ **A copy of the contest poster from Izzy's Ice Cream Parlor is important because it helps the reader understand _____**

    **A**    how many essays have been entered in the contest

    **B**    the criteria used to judge the essays

    **C**    why Izzy is sponsoring the contest

    **D**    who is the best father

Common Core Standard RI.5.9; Common Core Standard RL.5.9

☐ **What could have happened to the Father's Day celebration if President Calvin Coolidge had not proclaimed the third Sunday in June as Father's Day? Use details from the passage to support your response.**

_____

_____

_____

_____

_____

**Common Core Standard RI.5.5**

☐    In paragraph 1, why did Jeremy, Ontario, and Louisa want to enter the contest?

    **A**    They believe they have the best fathers.

    **B**    They want to win a prize.

    **C**    They like to eat sundaes at Izzy's Ice Cream Parlor.

    **D**    They believe they can win because they like to write stories and poetry.

---

**Common Core Standard RI.5.5**

☐    Why did Sonora Dodd wanted to honor her father?  Use details from the passage to support your response.

_____

_____

_____

_____

_____

---

**Common Core Standard RI.5.5**

☐    Why must each entry to the contest include a photo of the dad featured in the essay?

    **A**    Izzy wants to see if he knows the dads.

    **B**    Photos of the winners of the contest and their dads will appear in the local newspaper.

    **C**    Izzy wants to make sure each essay is about a real dad.

    **D**    The pictures of the winning dads will be on posters in the ice cream parlor.

**NOTE:** Use "Who will win the essay contest?" and "What is Celebrated on *Dia de los Muertos*?" to answer the next three questions.

Common Core Standard RL.5.9

☐ **One way these selections are alike is that both mention _____**

    **A    a celebration for deceased family members**

    **B    a holiday that is over 75 years old**

    **C    a special festival for children**

    **D    how a holiday was almost discontinued**

Common Core Standard RL.5.9

☐ **What is one difference between the two holidays?   Use details from the passage to support your response.**

_____

_____

_____

_____

_____

Common Core Standard RL.5.9

☐ **Both selections tell how _____**

    **A    to create a new holiday**

    **B    different cultures honor fathers on a Sunday**

    **C    visitors can participate in the holiday festivities**

    **D    a special holiday began**

PRACTICE

Name _____

Common Core Standard RI.5.1

☐   Look at this web of information.  Which of these belongs in the empty circle?

A    Judged by Izzy

B    At least 300 words in essay

C    Held annually

D    Four prizes

Announce winners on June 3rd

Must include photo of entrant with father

Father's Day Essay Contest

Entry deadline is June 1st

Common Core Standard RI.5.1

☐   Read the following diagram which shows some details from the passage.  Which detail belongs in the empty box?

Louisa's Dad

Gets up early on Saturday

Goes to college at night

Never misses her soccer games

A    Makes pancakes every morning

B    Coaches a basketball team

C    Likes baseball

D    Works all day

Common Core Standard RI.5.1

☐   Look at the diagram of information from the passage.  Which of these belongs in the blank?

Ontario's Dad
• Teaches school
• Helps Ontario with his homework
• Likes sports

Jeremy's Dad
• _____
• Pitches with Jeremy

A    Coaches church basketball team

B    Is very special

C    Goes to college at night

D    Makes pancakes

© Teachers' Treasures Publishing

Page 31

Name _____

---

Common Core Standard RL.5.1

☐ **From what the reader learns about Sonora Dodd, which statement does not make sense?**

A      She believed her father had worked hard to raise six children.

B      She chose June to honor all fathers because her father's birthday was in June.

C      She wanted national recognition for creating Father's Day.

D      She was not the first person who wanted to honor fathers with a special day.

---

Common Core Standard RL.5.1

☐ **From what the reader learns about Mr. Washburn, which statement does not make sense?**

A      He does not believe any of his students will win the essay contest.

B      He wanted his students to enter the essay contest because it would give them experience writing essays.

C      He was glad that Jeremy, Ontario, and Louisa had told him about the essay contest.

D      He wanted Izzy to be aware that all of his students would be entering the essay contest.

---

Common Core Standard RL.5.1

☐ **From what the reader learns about the essay contest, which statement makes sense?**

A      The contest has a total of $300 in cash prizes.

B      The contest is held each year before Father's Day.

C      There is no age limit for the essay contest.

D      The winners of the essay contest will be announced two weeks before Father's Day.

---

Name _____

---

Common Core Standard RI.5.8

☐ **The author probably wrote this selection to ____**

A    inform readers about Mr. Washburn's assignment for his class

B    entertain readers with a story about Father's Day

C    explain how to enter an essay contest

D    give readers information about how to write an essay

---

Common Core Standard RI.5.8

☐ **The author probably included a copy of one of the essay contest posters because ____**

A    the students in Mr. Washburn's class need to know how to enter the contest

B    Izzy gave one of the posters to Mr. Washburn

C    a reader might want to enter the contest

D    it gives information about the contest

---

Common Core Standard RI.5.8

☐ **The author probably included the article about the history of Father's Day because ____**

A    it explains how Father's Day was started

B    it gives readers information about Sonora Dodd

C    it entertains readers with a story about three friends

D    it stresses the importance of a presidential proclamation

---

**NOTE:** Use "Who will win the essay contest?" and "What is Celebrated on *Dia de los Muertos*?" to answer the next three questions.

Common Core Standard RI.5.7; Common Core Standard RL.5.9

☐ **How are the two selections alike? Use details from the passage to support your response.**

_____

_____

_____

_____

_____

Common Core Standard RI.5.3; Common Core Standard RL.5.9

☐ **How are the characters in the two selections different?**

A   The characters in "Who will win the essay contest?" will participate in a special holiday.

B   The characters in "What is Celebrated on *Dia de los Muertos*?" live in a large country.

C   Some of the characters in "Who will win the essay contest?" are fictional.

D   The characters in "What is Celebrated on *Dia de los Muertos*?" lived long *ago.*

Common Core Standard RL.5.9

☐ **How are the two selections different? Use details from the passage to support your response.**

_____

_____

_____

_____

_____

**Name** _____

Common Core Standard RI.5.8

☐ **Jeremy, Louisa, and Ontario would probably have entered the essay contest even if Mr. Washburn had not made it an assignment for the class because _____**

**A** their dads were special

**B** they each thought they could win the contest

**C** they had seen the poster in Izzy's Ice Cream Parlor

**D** they thought it would be fun

Common Core Standard RI.5.8

☐ **What can the reader tell about Sonora Dodd's father from information in the article "Father's Day History?"**

**A** He wanted her to create a special day for all fathers.

**B** He made his children work on the farm.

**C** He had to be a mother and a father to his six children.

**D** He wanted President Calvin Coolidge to order all states to celebrate Father's Day.

Common Core Standard RI.5.8

☐ **What can the reader tell about the essay contest?**

**A** There will be three prizes awarded in each age category.

**B** Most of the entrants will be from Mr. Washburn's class.

**C** Izzy will keep the essays and send them to a magazine.

**D** Most of the essays will be 100 words in length.

Common Core Standard RL.5.6

☐    **Which of these is an OPINION in this selection?**

A    In 1924 President Calvin Coolidge proclaimed the third Sunday in June as Father's Day.

B    Mr. Washburn went to the ice cream parlor and told Izzy, the owner, about the students' assignment.

C    Roses are the Father's Day flower.

D    Since they like to write stories and poetry, they knew this was something they had a good chance of winning.

Common Core Standard RL.5.6

☐    **Which of these is a FACT in this passage?**

A    This contest is the perfect opportunity for you to tell all the world why your dad is so wonderful!

B    Essays and pictures become the property of Izzy's Ice Cream Parlor and will not be returned.

C    It was her father that made all the parental sacrifices and was, in her eyes, a courageous, selfless, and loving man.

D    It was Sonora's efforts, however, that eventually led to a national observance.

Common Core Standard RL.5.6

☐    **Which of these is an OPINION in this passage?**

A    When he asked the students how Father's Day came into being, none of the students had an answer.

B    The next day at school they told their teacher, Mr. Washburn, about the contest.

C    Mr. Washburn thought it would be an interesting assignment for all of his students.

D    Winners will be announced June 3rd.

**Name** _____

Common Core Standard RL.5.3

☐ Which sentence from the selection shows that Izzy is pleased that Mr. Washburn wants his students to enter the essay contest?

A *Mr. Washburn went to the ice cream parlor and told Izzy, the owner, about the students' assignment.*

B *Izzy gave Mr. Washburn one of the posters that he had displayed on the windows so the students could follow the rules of the contest.*

C *Jeremy, Ontario, and Louisa were enjoying chocolate sundaes at Izzy's Ice Cream Parlor when they noticed a poster advertising an upcoming Father's Day Essay Contest.*

D *Essays and pictures become the property of Izzy's Ice Cream Parlor and will not be returned.*

Common Core Standard RL.5.1; Common Core Standard RL.5.3

☐ Which sentence from the selection shows the reader that the essay contest will be fair for all entrants?

A *Your essay should focus on what makes your dad deserve the title "Father of the Year."*

B *Pictures of all essay winners and their dads, as well as their essays, will appear in <u>The Local News</u> on Father's Day, June 11!*

C *Winners will be announced June 3$^{rd}$.*

D *Three winners will be selected in each of the following categories: 7-9; 10-12; 13-15.*

Common Core Standard RL.5.1; Common Core Standard RL.5.3

☐ Which sentence from the passage shows that Louisa thinks her essay will win first prize?

A *"Your entry will have to compete against mine," Louisa replied half jokingly.*

B *"My dad gets up early on Saturday and makes pancakes for us."*

C *"He never misses one of my soccer games and, also, goes to college at night after he has worked all day."*

D *Since they like to write stories and poetry, they knew this was something they had a good chance of winning.*

> **NOTE:** Use "Who will win the essay contest?" and "What is Celebrated on *Dia de los Muertos*?" to answer the next three questions

Common Core Standard RI.5.5; Common Core Standard RI.5.9

☐ The reader can tell that the selection "Who will win the essay contest?" is different from "What is Celebrated on *Dia de los Muertos*?" because _____

A    it tells about the beginning of a holiday

B    the holiday is still celebrated

C    the only facts about the holiday are found in "Father's Day History"

D    the main characters are not deceased

Common Core Standard RI.5.2; Common Core Standard RI.5.5; Common Core Standard RL.5.6

☐ An idea present in both selections is _____

A    students should learn about holidays

B    family members are very important

C    holidays should be celebrated with food

D    all holidays should be national holidays

Common Core Standard RI.5.5; Common Core Standard RI.5.9

☐ How are these two selections alike?

A    They give the history of a special holiday.

B    They tell about a holiday that is changing each year.

C    They have characters who want to win a contest.

D    They were written by a person who is afraid of death.

**Name** _____

Common Core Standard RI.5.3, Common Core Standard RL.5.3

☐ **If you were to write about someone special, who would you write about? Describe why this person is special to you in your response. Be sure to be creative and elaborate in your response.**

_____

_____

_____

_____

_____

_____

_____

_____

_____

_____

_____

_____

_____

_____

_____

_____

_____

_____

_____

_____

_____

_____

Name _____

# The Election

The fifth grade student council election is scheduled for Tuesday. Hannah and Drew are <u>running</u> for student council president. Roberto knew Hannah and Drew were nervous because they were <u>jumpy</u> and much too quiet.

Roberto is <u>undecided</u> on who will get his vote. Hannah lives next door to him, and they have been friends all of their lives. Drew is also a good friend, and he even played second base on Roberto's baseball team last summer.

Roberto has spent a lot of time contemplating who will get his vote. He decided to <u>review</u> each of their campaign posters before making his final decision.

---

## VOTE FOR HARD-WORKING HANNAH

"I will work <u>diligently</u> to get fifth graders the things they need."

President of Choir Club Last Year ● Office Aide This Year

If elected Hannah will work to –

* Reduce ice cream prices to 50 cents!
* Get more computer lab time for YOU!
* Set up a shared reading time so fifth graders can read to kindergarten kids!
* Have a fifth grade <u>fling</u> in the spring!

Vote on September 10 for a president who will work for YOU!

---

## DREW WILL ROCK IF HE CAN EARN THE SPOT!

### Cast your vote for DREW!
### You will not regret it!

DREW wants to –

- Increase Friday recess by 10 minutes.
- Reward students who turn in all homework assignments each grading period with an ice cream party.
- Conduct a fundraiser throughout the year so the fifth grade students can go to Seaworld at the end of the year.

DREW is prepared to work hard to be the best Student Council President

### EVER!!!
Please give him your vote!

VOTE for DREW!!    VOTE for DREW!!    VOTE for DREW!!    VOTE for DREW!!

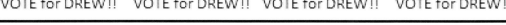

Name _____

**Common Core Standard RI.5.4; Common Core Standard RL.5.4**

☐   **In this passage, the word <u>running</u> means _____**

A      entering a relay race

B      exercise

C      pouring out

D      taking part in an election

**Common Core Standard RI.5.4; Common Core Standard RL.5.4**

☐   **The word <u>fling</u> in this passage means _____**

A      to toss away

B      test

C      celebration

D      holiday

**Common Core Standard RI.5.4; Common Core Standard RL.5.4**

☐   **In this passage, the word <u>jumpy</u> means_____**

A      leaping

B      anxious

C      angry

D      sad

Common Core Standard RI.4.4, Common Core Standard RL.4.4

☐    The word <u>diligently</u> in this passage means _____

A    everyday

B    tirelessly

C    for the fifth grade

D    carelessly

Common Core Standard RI.4.4, Common Core Standard RL.4.4

☐    In this passage, the word <u>undecided</u> means _____

A    knows

B    tell in advance

C    confident

D    uncertain

Common Core Standard RI.4.4, Common Core Standard RL.4.4

☐    The word <u>review</u> in this passage means _____

A    study

B    show others

C    complain

D    state again

Common Core Standard RI.5.5; Common Core Standard RL.5.1

☐ **Drew's campaign poster mentions that before students will be able to go to Seaworld, they will need to _____**

**A** do their homework

**B** prepare their lunches

**C** call him

**D** raise money

Common Core Standard RL.5.1

☐ **When did Hannah have experience as president of an organization?**

**A** This year

**B** While in the fourth grade

**C** In September

**D** On Tuesday

Common Core Standard RL.5.1

☐ **Which of these happened last in the passage?**

**A** Hannah created her campaign posters.

**B** Drew played baseball on Roberto's team.

**C** Roberto read the campaign posters again.

**D** Roberto knew they both were nervous.

**Common Core Standard RI.5.2; Common Core Standard RL.5.3**

☐ **Roberto is unsure which candidate to vote for because he _____**

A    does not think either one will do a good job

B    is friends with both candidates

C    does not care who wins

D    wanted to run for student council president

**Common Core Standard RI.5.3**

☐ **If elected, both candidates promise to _____**

A    increase recess time

B    reduce ice cream prices

C    go to Seaworld

D    work hard as president

**Common Core Standard RI.5.2**

☐ **The position of student council president will last for _____**

A    one week

B    one day

C    one school year

D    one month

Common Core Standard RL.5.7; Common Core Standard RL.5.1

☐    **Where will Roberto read the campaign posters?**

    A     **The baseball field**

    B     **His house**

    C     **At school**

    D     **The amusement park**

---

Common Core Standard RL.5.7; Common Core Standard RL.5.1

☐    **Where will the class go at the end of the year if Drew is elected?**

    A     **Six Flag over Texas**

    B     **Seaworld**

    C     **Disneyland**

    D     **Water World**

---

Common Core Standard RL.5.7; Common Core Standard RL.5.1

☐    **Where does Hannah work this year?**

    A     **Cafeteria**

    B     **Library**

    C     **Music room**

    D     **Office**

Name _____

Common Core Standard RL.5.7

☐ **What does Hannah want to do for her fifth grade classmates?**

A   Raise money for a party

B   Reduce ice cream prices

C   Have an ice cream party

D   Eliminate homework

Common Core Standard RL.5.7

☐ **How does Hannah's campaign poster describe her?  Use details from the passage to support your response.**

_____

_____

_____

_____

_____

_____

Common Core Standard RL.5.7

☐ **What does Drew promise will happen if you vote for him?**

A   You will not regret voting for him.

B   You will have more time in the computer lab.

C   You will not have any more homework.

D   You will read to kindergarten students.

**Name** _____

---

Common Core Standard RI.5.2

☐ **What is the first paragraph of this passage mainly about?**

A     Drew's campaign

B     Roberto's decision

C     The candidates for student council president

D     Hannah's best friend

---

Common Core Standard RI.5.2

☐ **What is the main idea of Drew's poster?**

A     He is smarter than Hannah.

B     He will win.

C     You will like him.

D     He is the best candidate for the job.

---

Common Core Standard RI.5.2

☐ **What is the main idea of Hannah's poster?**

A     She is prettier than Drew.

B     She will work hard as president.

C     She will vote on September 10.

D     She is in the fifth grade.

---

Name _____

Common Core Standard RL.5.2

☐ **Which is the best summary of this passage?**

A     Hannah lives next door to Roberto.

B     Roberto is having difficulty deciding between the two candidates for student council president.

C     Roberto will read the campaign posters.

D     Drew and Roberto are friends who played baseball on the same team.

Common Core Standard RL.5.2

☐ **What is the best summary of Hannah's campaign poster?**

A     She will not work on the weekends.

B     She will help fifth graders earn money for a trip.

C     She will help students get to know younger students on their campus.

D     She will work very hard to get things fifth grade students want and need.

Common Core Standard RL.5.2

☐ **Which is the best summary of Drew's campaign poster?**

A     He wants to go to Seaworld.

B     He does not like to do homework.

C     He wants your vote for president.

D     He will rock.

Common Core Standard RI.5.3; Common Core Standard RL.5.5

[ ]     **Drew might think Roberto will vote for him because they _____**

    **A     live next door to each other**

    **B     played on the same baseball team**

    **C     are in the fifth grade**

    **D     are boys**

Common Core Standard RI.5.3; Common Core Standard RL.5.5

[ ]     **Drew and Hannah made campaign posters because they were _____**

    **A     good artists**

    **B     good candidates**

    **C     candidates in an election**

    **D     going to win the race**

Common Core Standard RI.5.3; Common Core Standard RL.5.5

[ ]     **Hannah and Drew were acting strangely because _____**

    **A     they were sleepy**

    **B     they were angry**

    **C     they were too quiet**

    **D     they were nervous**

Common Core Standard RI.5.8

☐ **Both candidates hope to _____**

    A     conduct a fundraiser

    B     make the year better for fifth graders

    C     do away with homework

    D     listen to their classmates

Common Core Standard RI.5.8

☐ **What will probably happen next in this passage?**

    A     Hannah will win the election.

    B     The class will have a party.

    C     Roberto will vote.

    D     Roberto will make his decision.

Common Core Standard RI.5.8

☐ **Drew probably wants to reward students who do their homework because he _____**

    A     does his homework

    B     wants to beat Hannah

    C     thinks homework is important

    D     likes his teachers

PRACTICE

Name _____

Common Core Standard RL.5.3; Common Core Standard RL.5.9

☐ **Which candidate thinks reading is important?**

A    Drew

B    Drew and Hannah

C    Hannah

D    Roberto

Common Core Standard RL.5.3; Common Core Standard RL.5.9

☐ **Hannah and Drew are probably nervous because _____**

A    of the upcoming election

B    Roberto has not decided who he will cast his vote fot

C    they made a lot of campaign posters

D    their teacher is angry

Common Core Standard RI.4.5

☐ **When the election is over, Hannah and Drew will probably feel _____**

A    sad

B    relieved

C    frustrated

D    angry

Common Core Standard RI.5.3; Common Core Standard RL.5.9

☐ **According to the passage, how are Hannah and Drew's campaign promises alike?**

A    They want to reduce ice cream prices.

B    They want to reward students who do their homework.

C    They have been president of an organization.

D    They want to have a special event for the students.

Common Core Standard RI.5.8; Common Core Standard RL.5.9

☐ **Why is Roberto probably having difficulty selecting a candidate to vote for?**

A    He lives next door to both candidates.

B    He believes both candidates will do a good job.

C    He likes Drew better than Hannah.

D    He is never able to make up his mind on an issue.

Common Core Standard RI.5.8; Common Core Standard RL.5.9

☐ **What qualifications does Hannah have that Drew does not?**

A    She is in the fifth grade.

B    She lives next door to Roberto.

C    She has been president of a club.

D    She is a girl.

Common Core Standard RI.5.9

☐ **Who will probably need to approve the changes before they can happen on Hannah and Drew's campaign posters?**

A    The coach

B    The principal

C    Their parents

D    The fifth grade students

Common Core Standard RI.5.9

☐ **You can tell from this passage that Roberto probably will _____**

A    have difficulty deciding who to vote for in the election

B    chose not to vote in the election

C    talk to Hannah about why he did not vote for her

D    vote for Drew because they were baseball teammates

Common Core Standard RI.5.9

☐ **Information in the passage suggests that _____**

A    Roberto is not a very good friend

B    Drew thinks he will win

C    Hannah may be a better president because she has had experience as president of a club

D    Roberto will decide to run against both of them

Common Core Standard RI.5.3; Common Core Standard RL.5.3

☐ **How will Drew probably feel if he does not win the election?**

    **A**    Angry

    **B**    Irritated

    **C**    Happy

    **D**    Defeated

Common Core Standard RI.5.3; Common Core Standard RL.5.3

☐ **How could Hannah and Drew's attitudes be described before the election?**

    **A**    Competitive

    **B**    Angry

    **C**    Joyful

    **D**    Funny

Common Core Standard RI.5.3; Common Core Standard RL.5.3

☐ **Information in Drew's campaign poster suggests that _____**

    **A**    Roberto thinks Drew is the best candidate

    **B**    Drew thinks he is the best candidate

    **C**    everyone wants to be student council president

    **D**    Hannah thinks Drew is the best candidate

Name _____

Common Core Standard RI.5.6; Common Core Standard RI.5.9

☐ How would Roberto's problem probably have been different if the candidates were not Hannah and Drew?

A    He could have entered the race.

B    He would not have voted.

C    He might not have been choosing between two good friends.

D    He would have voted for the boy candidate.

Common Core Standard RI.5.6; Common Core Standard RI.5.9

☐ What would probably be different if the students were electing class homecoming queen instead of student council president?

A    Hannah would not have been a candidate.

B    Drew would not have been a candidate.

C    The election would have been in the summer.

D    Roberto would have been a candidate.

Common Core Standard RI.5.6; Common Core Standard RI.5.9

☐ The students will probably cast their votes _____

A    at home

B    in the cafeteria

C    on the football field

D    in their classroom

Common Core Standard RI.5.7

☐ **According to the posters, when will the election take place?**

    A     Friday, September 10

    B     Tuesday, September 9

    C     Tuesday, September 10

    D     Tuesday, October 10

Common Core Standard RI.5.7; Common Core Standard RL.5.7

☐ **You can tell from the posters that the candidates are mainly concerned about ____**

    A     their grades

    B     the cost of desserts

    C     having a party

    D     helping their classmates

Common Core Standard RI.5.7

☐ **Which of these statements is best supported by information in the passage?**

    A     Hannah and Drew do not like each other.

    B     Both of the candidates will do a good job for their classmates.

    C     Roberto has made a decision on who he will vote for.

    D     The candidates spent a lot of money on their campaigns.

Common Core Standard RI.5.9; Common Core Standard RL.5.7

☐     **Information on Drew's poster suggests that** _____

    **A**     he does not want to win

    **B**     he is eager to be elected

    **C**     he thinks Hannah will win

    **D**     he thinks this job is not very important

Common Core Standard RI.5.9; Common Core Standard RL.5.7

☐     **After Roberto reads the campaign posters again, he will probably** _____

    **A**     decide he should enter the race

    **B**     go home

    **C**     make his decision

    **D**     ask Drew for his opinion

Common Core Standard RI.5.9

☐     **After the election, Hannah will probably** _____

    **A**     have a party

    **B**     talk to Roberto about who he voted for

    **C**     write a letter to Drew

    **D**     not be nervous anymore

Common Core Standard RL.5.6

☐　　**Which is a FACT stated in this passage?**

A　　Roberto is prepared to be the best student council president ever.

B　　Hannah was president of the Choir Club last year.

C　　Roberto is a talented second baseman.

D　　Drew lives next door to Hannah.

Common Core Standard RL.5.6

☐　　**Which is an OPINION in this passage?**

A　　Drew wants to increase recess by 10 minutes.

B　　Student council elections will be held on Tuesday.

C　　Roberto is undecided about who to vote for.

D　　Hannah is hard working.

Common Core Standard RL.5.6

☐　　**Which is an OPINION in this passage?**

A　　Roberto knew Hannah and Drew were nervous.

B　　Hannah is working in the office this year.

C　　Roberto wants to reread the campaign posters.

D　　Drew wants everyone to vote for him.

**Name** _____

---

Common Core Standard RL.5.2

☐     Hannah probably listed her campaign promises on the poster so that _____

    A     the students would have a lot to read

    B     the students would know when to vote

    C     the students would know how she plans to improve their year

    D     Roberto could read them

---

Common Core Standard RL.5.2

☐     What was the author's purpose for writing this passage?

    A     To describe Hannah

    B     To inform the reader about the student council president elections

    C     To tell a story about a president

    D     To explain how to vote

---

Common Core Standard RL.5.2

☐     The candidates probably made campaign posters so that _____

    A     the students could decide who will be the best president

    B     they could show off their writing skills

    C     Roberto would have a problem

    D     the students would contribute money to their campaigns

---

**Name** _____

Common Core Standard RL.5.6

☐  The writer of this passage thinks that choosing between friends is ____

A    troublesome

B    easy

C    thrilling

D    tiring

Common Core Standard RL.5.6

☐  The author of this passage probably believes ____

A    Hannah should win

B    Drew should win

C    choosing a candidate is a good experience for students

D    the school should eliminate elections

Common Core Standard RL.5.6

☐  The author of this passage seems to think ____

A    there is no need to have school elections

B    the students will have a hard decision deciding between the two candidates

C    only adults should vote

D    the students should not vote if they are undecided

**Name** _____

Common Core Standard RI.5.3, Common Core Standard RL.5.3

☐    **If you had to vote for either Hannah or Drew, who would you vote for? Explain why you chose that person in your response.  Use details from the passage to support your response.**

_____

_____

_____

_____

_____

_____

_____

_____

_____

_____

_____

_____

_____

_____

_____

_____

_____

_____

_____

_____

_____

_____

# Manatees: Gentle Giants

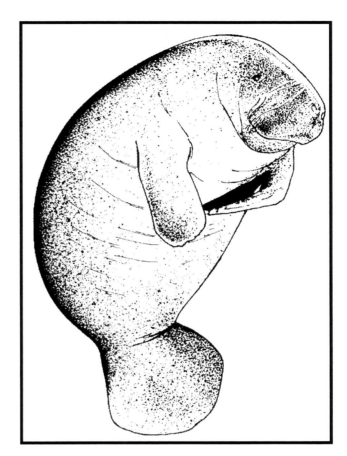

1    Manatees are interesting underwater creatures. They are large, gentle animals that spend their whole lives in the water. They are sometimes called "sea cows" or "river cows" because, like cows, they are vegetarians and only feed on plant life found in the ocean. They can consume as much as 100 to 150 pounds of food per day. The manatees usually weigh more than 1000 pounds and can grow to a length of about 12 feet. These <u>harmless</u>, happy marine mammals swim through the oceans in warm climates such as Florida and California. For some manatees, finding warm waters is a matter of <u>survival</u>, because to stay in the cold waters could mean catching a breathing illness, the most common natural cause of death.

2    Manatees have existed for more than 60 million years which means they were around at the same time as the dinosaurs. Although manatees look like many animals, scientists believe manatees and elephants actually are related. The most outstanding similarities between these two include their toenails, teeth, digestive tract, mouth parts, skin, and hair. All of these add to the evidence supporting the theory that elephants and manatees have common ancestors.

## Characteristics of Manatees

3    Manatees look like a combination of several animals. Manatees have a shape much like a seal. Their large body tapers to a powerful, flat tail that helps them swim. The manatee has two flexible forelimbs which act like arms to help them maneuver in shallow water, grasp and move food toward their mouths, and act like flippers during swimming. Their broad, whiskered faces look like the face of a walrus. The rough, gray skin that covers their body is similar to the <u>hide</u> of an elephant. Their skin reacts to touch because their bodies are very muscular, contracting and changing shape slightly when scratched or tickled. They usually swim slowly and sometimes creep along the bottom with their flippers.

4    Manatees give birth to only one calf every three to five years. A newborn calf is pinkish, about four feet long, and weighs 60 to 100 pounds, about as big as a full grown goat. Once born, a calf immediately swims to the surface for its first breath of air. Sometimes a calf grips or rests on its mother's back as she feeds or sleeps and comes up to the surface for air when she does. Though the calf is able to eat plants soon after its birth, it drinks milk from its mother for up to two years. The father does not participate in the care of the calf. The mother and father do not stay together as a pair.

## Food and Breathing

5    Manatees are *herbivores* which means they only eat plants. Manatees eat sea grass and other saltwater plants as they slowly paddle along in the ocean. Although manatees mainly eat larger

aquatic plants, they also eat algae and crustacea. Manatees spend more time feeding just before winter because they need more energy to maintain their body temperature in colder water. Because manatees are so enormous, they sometimes spend about six to eight hours a day eating. Its teeth are broad and flat, well suited for grinding plants; however, they have no front teeth. They eat such a great quantity of food that their teeth can actually be worn away because of so much chewing. However, new teeth that have formed at the back of the jaw move forward and push the old ones out.

6    Manatees take a lot of rest breaks when they are eating. While they are resting, they usually doze just below the water's surface or by lying on the bottom. Their noses are on top of their faces for easy breathing so, although they can hold their breath for as long as 20 minutes, they must always come to the surface for a quick breath. Amazingly, they can do this without even waking up!

### Eyes, Ears, and Communication

7    The manatee's eyes seem tiny for such a large mammal, but it is believed they have excellent close vision. This makes sense because manatees spend so much time in waters that are muddy and cloudy. Their eyes can be blue or brown, and they can identify colors.

8    Manatees have no external ears, but they can hear very well. Their <u>organ</u> of hearing is a tiny hole just behind their eyes. These work well underwater, since sound travels six times better in water than in air. However, it is difficult to know where sound is coming from when under water, so they may not be able to tell where boat motor sounds are coming from. This could be one reason manatees are often struck by boat propellers.

9    Manatees make sounds such as squeaks and squeals when frightened, playing, or between a cow and a calf. No air is released from the manatee when these sounds are made, and it is not clear where the sounds are being reproduced or if they serve any other purpose.

### Social Behavior

10    Manatees are not possessive about territory like other animals such as dogs. They are not aggressive in any way and do not fight with each other. They are extremely gentle animals. Because they have no natural enemies, manatees do not need to travel in large herds which offer protection to the members of the group. Individual manatees form groups that do not have a leader. Manatees engage in social activities such as chasing, bumping, and sometimes body surfing together. They grab each other's flippers, put their mouths together, and nibble and kiss gently to greet each other.

### Their Future

11    There is reason to be concerned about the manatee's future, but they can be saved in spite of all of the dangers they face. Conservation groups are working to enforce laws forbidding the hunting of manatees. They are also working with the government to establish places of safety where manatees can live <u>undisturbed</u> by hunters, boats, and pollution. Manatees are currently an endangered species because of hunting and water pollution, but most die from boat propellers. Hopefully, now that manatees are recognized as an endangered species, people will do a better job of protecting them to ensure that this special mammal survives extinction.

# A Veterinarian's Story of the Rescue of an Injured Manatee

12      Dr. Lowe is a veterinarian at a wildlife park where he is responsible for the care of nine manatees that live at the park. The park is a shelter for injured or orphaned manatees who need treatment at a critical care facility. They are housed, fed, and cared for until their release or for the rest of their lives. This is an account of an injured manatee that was brought to the park for care.

13      *Dr. Lowe started assessing the injuries, <u>dressing</u> the wound, and taking needed blood samples. He found that the manatee had a collapsed lung, several broken ribs, air in the chest cavity, and a gash approximately five inches deep and eight inches long across its back, dangerously close to its spinal column.*

14      *Dr. Lowe said the collapsed lung was probably caused by one of the broken ribs, which most likely occurred when a boat hit the manatee causing a crushing type injury. One cut from a propeller blade was especially deep, and looked as if it may have affected the spinal column. He said it appeared the animal had been injured several days before because the smaller cuts had already started to heal. However, the internal injuries of the manatee were of greater concern. It seemed almost impossible that the manatee had been struck twice, one strike resulting in the punctured lung and broken ribs, and the next strike resulting in the propeller cuts when the animal was unable to avoid a second boat due to its injuries.*

15      *The manatee was lifted from a boat and moved into the rescue trailer for transport to a critical care facility. A special stretcher was used to move the animal, then foam pads and supports were used to position the manatee within the trailer.*

16      *Dr. Lowe said the animal was in considerable pain from its injuries, but it would most likely survive.*

17      *After examining the manatee it appeared the spinal column was intact and the animal still had feeling throughout its body. However, Dr. Lowe found a severe infection, 9 fractured ribs, and multiple fractures.*

Name _____

Common Core Standard RI.5.4; Common Core Standard RL.5.4

☐   **Read the meanings below for the word hide.**

**Which meaning best fits the way hide is used in paragraph 3?**

A    Meaning 3

B    Meaning 1

C    Meaning 4

D    Meaning 2

> hide ('hīd) *noun*
> 1. the skin of an animal whether fresh or prepared for use
> *verb*
> 2. to put or stay out of sight
> 3. to keep secret
> 4. to screen from view

Common Core Standard RI.5.4; Common Core Standard RL.5.4

☐   **Read the meanings below for the word organ.**

**Which meaning best fits the way organ is used in paragraph 8?**

A    Meaning 2

B    Meaning 3

C    Meaning 1

D    Meaning 4

> organ ('or-gen) *noun*
> 1. a musical instrument played by means of one or more keyboards and having pipes
> 2. a part of a person, plant, or animal that is specialized to do a particular task
> 3. a way of getting something done
> 4. a periodical

Common Core Standard RI.5.4; Common Core Standard RL.5.4

☐   **Read the meanings below for the word dressing.**

**Which meaning best fits the way dressing is used in paragraph 13?**

A    Meaning 3

B    Meaning 2

C    Meaning 4

D    Meaning 1

> dressing ('dres-ing) *noun*
> 1. the act or process of one who dresses
> 2. a sauce added to a food
> 3. a seasoned mixture used as a stuffing
> 4. a material used to cover an injury

Name _____

---

Common Core Standard RI.5.4; Common Core Standard RL.5.4

☐    **In paragraph 1, the word <u>harmless</u> means _____**

    A    extremely large

    B    vicious

    C    safe

    D    uninjured

---

Common Core Standard RI.5.4; Common Core Standard RL.5.4

☐    **In paragraph 1, the word <u>survival</u> means _____**

    A    convenience

    B    continue to exist

    C    in danger

    D    a long life

---

Common Core Standard RI.5.4; Common Core Standard RL.5.4

☐    **In paragraph 11, the word <u>undisturbed</u> means _____**

    A    without interruption

    B    in their home

    C    angry

    D    asleep

---

**Name** _____

---

Common Core Standard RI.5.2

☐ **Paragraph 11 is mainly about** _____

   A   how manatees die from hunters, boats, and pollution

   B   government agencies

   C   encouraging people to save manatees

   D   efforts to save the manatee from extinction

---

Common Core Standard RI.5.2

☐ **According to the passage, there is a reason to be concerned about the manatees' future because** _____

   A   conservation groups are working to enforce the laws

   B   manatees only eat plants

   C   manatees are currently an endangered species

   D   manatees look like a combination of several animals

---

Common Core Standard RI.5.2

☐ **Paragraph 12 is mainly about** _____

   A   a veterinarian

   B   a wildlife park where injured manatees live

   C   a manatee's rescue

   D   an account of an injured manatee

---

Name _____

Common Core Standard RI.5.7; Common Core Standard RL.5.1

☐    **Which of the following best completes the summary?**

> Summary of "A Veterinarian's Story of
> the Rescue of an Injured Manatee"
>
> Dr. Lowe began by assessing the
> injuries of a manatee that was injured by
> a boat propeller.
> _____
> _____
> _____

A    The manatee had many cuts, but the internal injuries were the most dangerous to the mammal.  It will live.

B    Dr. Lowe found serious wounds, but he was the most troubled by the internal injuries of the manatee.  After thoroughly examining the manatee, Dr. Lowe concluded that the manatee would probably live.

C    Dr. Lowe saw that the manatee had a collapsed lung, broken ribs, air in the chest cavity, and cuts of various sizes.  He believed that the manatee had been injured for several days because most of the wounds had already begun to heal.

D    After examining the manatee, Dr. Lowe treated the wounds and released the manatee back into the ocean.

**Name** _____

Common Core Standard RL.5.3

☐   **What can the reader tell about Dr. Lowe?**

    A     He is usually unable to save the life of injured manatees.

    B     He is an expert on the care of injured manatees.

    C     He believes every state should have a shelter for injured manatees.

    D     He does not like to work with large mammals.

Common Core Standard RL.5.3

☐   **The reader can tell that the manatee is _____**

    A     very large and aggressive

    B     a mammal that eats other mammals

    C     almost blind

    D     very large, but very gentle

Common Core Standard RI.5.5; Common Core Standard RL.5.3

☐   **Manatees can be found near Florida and California because _____**

    A     they are safe

    B     they like to swim in the ocean

    C     they can become ill if they stay in cold water

    D     there are many wildlife refuges

---

**Common Core Standard RI.5.5**

☐   **Dr. Lowe and his staff work at a wildlife park that is _____**

   A   located in Florida

   B   near an ocean with warm water

   C   famous

   D   situated on an island

---

**Common Core Standard RI.5.5**

☐   **Paragraph 1 is important because it helps the reader understand _____**

   A   how manatees and elephants are alike

   B   how a manatee swims

   C   how manatees eat

   D   why manatees should avoid cold climates

---

**Common Core Standard RI.5.5**

☐   **Paragraph 11 is important because it helps the reader understand _____**

   A   the ways manatees are being protected

   B   the laws protecting manatees

   C   what kind of boat propellers injure manatees

   D   the dangerous manatee

---

Common Core Standard RI.5.5

☐    **Manatees do not swim and travel in large groups because ____**

     A     they do not have a leader

     B     they are not aggressive

     C     they are very gentle

     D     they have no natural enemies

---

Common Core Standard RI.5.5; Common Core Standard RL.5.3

☐    **Look at the chart. Which idea belongs in the empty box?**

| **Cause** | | **Effect** |
|-----------|---|------------|
| | → | Manatees and elephants may have common ancestors. |

     A     They have similar toenails, teeth, digestive tract, mouth parts, skin, and hair.

     B     They have existed for more than 60 million years.

     C     They lived with the dinosaurs.

     D     They look like a combination of several animals.

---

Common Core Standard RI.5.5

☐    **Why do most manatees usually weigh more than 1000 pounds?**

     A     They are about 12 feet long.

     B     They are vegetarians and eat plant life found in the ocean.

     C     They eat about 100 to 150 pounds of food each day.

     D     They are sometimes called "sea cows" or "river cows."

**Common Core Standard RI.5.1**

☐    Look at this web of information.  Which of these belongs in the empty circle?

A    Social Behavior

B    Characteristics of Manatees

C    Food and Breathing

D    Eyes, Ears, and Communication

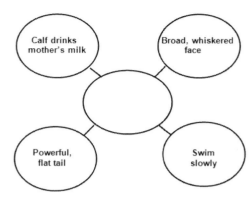

---

**Common Core Standard RI.5.1**

☐    Read this outline of information from the passage.  Which of the following belongs in the blank?

A    Not possessive about territory

B    Characteristics of Manatees

C    Their Future

D    Social Behavior

A.  Food and Breathing
   1.  Eat only plants
   2.  Noses on top of their faces
B.  Eyes, Ears, and Communication
   1.  Excellent close vision
   2.  Hear very well
   3.  Make squeaks and squeals
C.  _____
   1.  Not aggressive
   2.  Gently greet each other

---

**Common Core Standard RI.5.1**

☐    Look at the diagram of information from the passage.  Which of these belongs in the empty box?

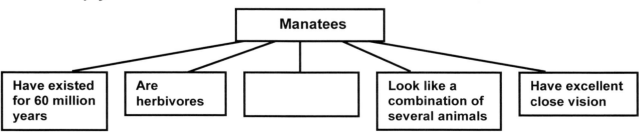

A    Live in state parks          C    Not possessive about territory

B    Eat fish                     D    Eat 1000 pounds of food per day

Name _____

Common Core Standard RL.5.1

☐ **From what the reader learns about manatees, which statement does not make sense?**

    A     Manatees are harmless, happy marine mammals.

    B     Manatees do not mate for life.

    C     Manatee calves drink their mother's milk because they are unable to eat.

    D     Manatees are large, gentle animals that spend their whole lives in the water.

Common Core Standard RI.5.7; Common Core Standard RL.5.1

☐ **From what the reader learns about the injured manatee, which statement does not make sense?**

    A     The injured manatee was in critical condition.

    B     The injured manatee's spine was damaged.

    C     The injured manatee had cuts from a boat propeller.

    D     The injured manatee would live.

Common Core Standard RI.5.7; Common Core Standard RL.5.1

☐ **From what the reader learns about manatees, which statement makes sense?**

    A     The rough, brown skin that covers a manatee's body is similar to the hide of an elephant.

    B     Manatees will fight each other over food.

    C     Manatees form groups with a leader.

    D     Manatees are playful.

---

**Common Core Standard RL.5.6**

☐ The author probably wrote this selection to _____

A influence the reader to protect manatees

B entertain readers with an account of how a manatee was saved

C inform the reader about an endangered species

D give the reader information about where to see a manatee

---

**Common Core Standard RL.5.6**

☐ The author of this selection is probably _____

A a veterinarian

B sympathetic to the dangers that manatees face

C a member of a conservation group

D Dr. Lowe's assistant

---

**Common Core Standard RL.5.6**

☐ The author probably included the section "A Veterinarian's Story of the Rescue of an Injured Manatee" because _____

A Dr. Lowe is a famous veterinarian

B the reader may want to visit the wildlife park

C most manatees will eventually come to the wildlife park

D it reinforces the idea that manatees can be seriously injured by boat propellers

---

**Name** _____

Common Core Standard RL.5.8

☐   The reader can tell from information in the passage that the author ____

A    has worked with manatees

B    thinks manatees are an interesting mammal

C    believes manatees should be extinct

D    fears the possible effects of manatees on the environment

---

Common Core Standard RL.5.8

☐   The author probably ____

A    wants the reader to become involved in the protection of manatees

B    believes most people do not understand manatees

C    wrote this selection after experiencing the rescue of a manatee

D    believes manatees should be protected

---

Common Core Standard RL.5.8

☐   In the selection the author probably ____

A    wants to make readers aware of how man is destroying a gentle mammal

B    has seen mammals in an ocean

C    wants readers to learn more about caring for injured manatees

D    wants to make readers aware of the efforts of Dr. Lowe to save manatees

**Name** _____

---

Common Core Standard RI.5.6

☐   Manatees probably swim very slowly because ____

    A    they are looking for plants to eat

    B    they can hold their breath for as long as 20 minutes

    C    they have no enemies

    D    they are very heavy

---

Common Core Standard RI.5.6

☐   What can the reader tell about manatees from information in the selection?

    A    Manatees are helpless when they encounter a boat propeller.

    B    Manatees abandon their young when they are two years old.

    C    Manatees and dinosaurs were enemies.

    D    Manatees would eat fish if they could swim fast enough to catch them.

---

Common Core Standard RI.5.6

☐   The reader can tell that manatees are gentle because ____

    A    they are not possessive

    B    they nibble and kiss gently to greet each other

    C    they spend their whole lives in the water

    D    they carry their young on their backs

---

**Common Core Standard RL.5.6**

☐ **Which of these is an OPINION in this selection?**

A Manatees give birth to only one calf every three to five years.

B Manatees are *herbivores* which means they only eat plants.

C Manatees are interesting underwater creatures.

D The father does not participate in the care of the calf.

---

**Common Core Standard RL.5.6**

☐ **Which of these is a FACT in this passage?**

A Manatees look like a combination of several animals.

B The mother and father do not stay together as a pair.

C They are extremely gentle animals.

D Manatees are not possessive about territory like other animals such as dogs.

---

**Common Core Standard RL.5.6**

☐ **Which of these is an OPINION in this passage?**

A Dr. Lowe said the animal was in considerable pain from its injuries, but it would most likely survive.

B The park is a shelter for injured or orphaned manatees who need treatment at a critical care facility.

C Their organ of hearing is a tiny hole just behind their eyes.

D Their eyes can be blue or brown, and they can identify colors

Name _____

---

Common Core Standard RI.5.7

☐     **Which sentence from the selection shows why manatees probably weigh more than 1000 pounds?**

    A     *Manatees eat sea grass and other saltwater plants as they slowly paddle along in the ocean.*

    B     *Manatees take a lot of rest breaks when they are eating.*

    C     *They are sometimes called "sea cows" or "river cows" because, like cows, they are vegetarians and only feed on plant life found in the ocean.*

    D     *They sometimes spend about six to eight hours a day eating.*

---

Common Core Standard RI.5.7

☐     **Which sentence from the selection shows the reader that a boat propeller can be dangerous to a manatee?**

    A     *Dr. Lowe started assessing the injuries, dressing the wound, and taking needed blood samples.*

    B     *He found that the manatee had a collapsed lung, several broken ribs, air in the chest cavity, and a gash approximately five inches deep and eight inches long across its back, dangerously close to its spinal column.*

    C     *Dr. Lowe is a veterinarian at a wildlife park where he is responsible for the care of nine manatees that live at the park.*

    D     *They are housed, fed, and cared for until their release or for the rest of their lives.*

---

Common Core Standard RI.5.7

☐     **Which sentence from the passage shows that manatees are probably a happy animal?**

    A     *Manatees take a lot of rest breaks when they are eating.*

    B     *They are not aggressive in any way and do not fight with each other.*

    C     *They grab each other's flippers, put their mouths together, and nibble and kiss gently to greet each other.*

    D     *They can consume as much as 100 to 150 pounds of food per day.*

---

**Name** _____

---

Common Core Standard RI.5.9

☐    The author of the passage "A Veterinarian's Story of the Rescue of an Injured Manatee" begins the passage with _____

    A    a story about an injured manatee

    B    information about Dr. Lowe and the wildlife park

    C    an explanation of how Dr. Lowe determines which manatees will stay at the wildlife park

    D    the name of the wildlife park

---

Common Core Standard RI.5.9

☐    The author of the article "Manatees: Gentle Giants" organized paragraphs 1 through 11 by _____

    A    using illustrations and pictures

    B    describing how a manatee was saved

    C    showing how manatees resemble other animals

    D    giving information about manatees under subtitles

---

Common Core Standard RI.5.9

☐    The purpose of paragraphs 1 and 2 are to _____

    A    show the relationship between manatees and dinosaurs

    B    create a picture of manatees in the reader's mind

    C    create an interest in manatees so the reader will want to know more about these mammals

    D    encourage the reader to assist in the protection of manatees

# The Tour de France

Every July more than 150 world class cyclists gather in Futuroscope, France, to compete in one of the most prestigious bicycle races in the world, the Tour de France.

This <u>physically</u> demanding race requires cyclists to travel a distance of about 2,255 miles of European roads over a <u>period</u> of twenty-five to thirty days. The course of the Tour changes each year. It lies mostly in France, but has also passed through Belgium, Spain, England, Ireland, Germany, and Switzerland. Cyclists travel through cities, villages, farmland, and mountain ranges as they make their way towards Paris, France, and a possible <u>victory</u>.

The Tour de France is a *stage* race, meaning it is divided into sections, or stages. There is a different <u>stage</u> almost every day. The average biking distance is about 100 miles per day. Some stages require a particular cycling skill, such as climbing hills, sprinting, or performance in time-trial races. Cyclists are timed for each stage. Throughout the race the cyclist in the lead at each stage gets to wear the *maillot jaune* (yellow jersey), and at the end of the race, the <u>privilege</u> is reserved, or saved, for the winner of the Tour.

There are other symbolic jerseys in the race including a green jersey for the fastest sprinter, and a white and polka-dot jersey for the best climber. However, none of these are as meaningful as the yellow jersey.

Each cyclist in the Tour belongs to a team of nine cyclists. The leader is the best all-around cyclist, and the other team members aid and support the leader during the race. The winner receives approximately $300,000 in prize money and the opportunity to wear the <u>symbolic</u> yellow jersey. The prize money is usually shared among the winning team members.

At the beginning of the race the course is <u>relatively</u> flat. However, <u>close</u> to the middle of the event, the cyclists are <u>challenged</u> by mountain ranges. Because of the grueling demands of the race, there are two rest days for the cyclists. Cyclists also take alternative forms of transportation at two locations. At the beginning of the race they travel by plane between Revel and Avignon, France. Near the end of the race they are transported by train from Troyes to Paris, France, where the winner, wearing his yellow jersey, does a victory lap at Champs-Elysees Avenue, a famous French landmark in Paris.

Common Core Standard RI.5.4; Common Core Standard RL.5.4

☐ **According to this passage, the word <u>period</u> means _____**

A    something new

B    a sentence

C    a space of time

D    to end

---

Common Core Standard RI.5.4; Common Core Standard RL.5.4

☐ **The word <u>close</u> in this passage means _____**

A    to shut

B    near

C    small

D    long

---

Common Core Standard RI.5.4; Common Core Standard RL.5.4

☐ **In this passage, the word <u>privilege</u> means _____**

A    something special

B    something well known

C    something debated

D    hard work

Common Core Standard RI.5.4; Common Core Standard RL.5.4

☐     In this passage, the word <u>relatively</u> means _____

A     more or less

B     extreme

C     family member

D     flat

Common Core Standard RI.5.4; Common Core Standard RL.5.4

☐     The word <u>challenged</u> in this passage means _____

A     made easy

B     fastest

C     made difficult

D     known about

Common Core Standard RI.5.4; Common Core Standard RL.5.4

☐     In this passage, the word <u>stage</u> means _____

A     the same

B     to present

C     a raised platform

D     a part of something

**Name** _____

---

Common Core Standard RI.5.4; Common Core Standard RL.5.4

☐   **In this passage, the word <u>physically</u> means _____**

    **A**    related to the mind

    **B**    related to the body

    **C**    related to sports

    **D**    hard

---

Common Core Standard RI.5.4; Common Core Standard RL.5.4

☐   **The word <u>victory</u> in this passage means _____**

    **A**    lose

    **B**    compete

    **C**    fast

    **D**    win

---

Common Core Standard RI.5.4; Common Core Standard RL.5.4

☐   **In this passage, the word <u>symbolic</u> means _____**

    **A**    against

    **B**    colorful

    **C**    stands for

    **D**    comfortable

---

**Common Core Standard RI.5.5**

☐     **At the beginning of the race, the course is fairly _____**

A     hilly

B     flat

C     long

D     steep

---

**Common Core Standard RI.5.5**

☐     **At the end of the race the winner _____**

A     does a victory lap

B     gives a speech

C     does a dance

D     has his picture taken in the symbolic yellow jersey

---

**Common Core Standard RI.5.5**

☐     **When do the cyclists travel over the mountains?**

A     At the beginning of the race

B     After the two day rest

C     About half-way through the race

D     At the end of the race

Name _____

Common Core Standard RI.5.1

☐    **The race starts in _____**

    **A**     Nantes

    **B**     London

    **C**     Futuroscope

    **D**     Paris

Common Core Standard RI.5.1

☐    **How are the cyclists transported to Paris at the end of the race?**

    **A**     Plane

    **B**     Train

    **C**     Car

    **D**     Bike

Common Core Standard RI.5.1

☐    **What color jerseys are awarded and how do cyclists earn them? Use details from the passage to support your response.**

_____

_____

_____

_____

_____

_____

Common Core Standard RI.5.7; Common Core Standard RL.5.1

☐    **The Tour de France takes place in ____**

   A      Australia

   B      The United States

   C      China

   D      Europe

Common Core Standard RI.5.7; Common Core Standard RL.5.1

☐    **At the end of the race the cyclists will arrive in ____**

   A      Futuroscope

   B      Paris

   C      Germany

   D      London

Common Core Standard RI.5.7; Common Core Standard RL.5.1

☐    **Which of the following is NOT a country that the cyclist will travel through?**

   A      United States

   B      France

   C      Germany

   D      Switzerland

**Name** _____

---

Common Core Standard RI.5.7

☐ **What is the team time trial numbered on the map?**

    **A**    **Two**

    **B**    **Four**

    **C**    **Six**

    **D**    **Eight**

---

Common Core Standard RI.5.7

☐ **Where will the cyclists spend their rest day on July 17?**

    **A**    **Courchevel**

    **B**    **Briancon**

    **C**    **Revel**

    **D**    **Nimes**

---

Common Core Standard RI.5.7; Common Core Standard RI.5.1

☐ **From what city will the cyclists leave on the plane transfer on the first rest day?**

    **A**    **Nimes**

    **B**    **Avignon**

    **C**    **Toulouse**

    **D**    **Revel**

---

Common Core Standard RI.5.2

☐    The main idea of the third paragraph is _____

A    the length of the race

B    who gets to wear the yellow jersey

C    the difference between racing and cycling

D    how the course is divided

Common Core Standard RI.5.2

☐    What is the main idea of this passage?

A    The Tour de France is a difficult race that challenges the professional cyclists in many ways.

B    The winner receives a yellow jersey.

C    The cyclists travel over mountains and flat lands.

D    The route of the race goes through many cities, small towns, and farmlands.

Common Core Standard RI.5.2; Common Core Standard RL.5.2

☐    What is this passage mostly about?

A    The demands of the race

B    An exciting and demanding world class bicycle race held in Europe

C    The prize money the winner receives

D    The length of the race in France

Name _____

Common Core Standard RI.5.2; Common Core Standard RL.5.2

☐ **Which is the best summary of this passage?**

A    The winner will receive $300,000 and a yellow jersey.

B    The Tour de France, the most celebrated bicycle race in the world, tests the skills of the cyclists as they travel over a challenging course.

C    Some of the cyclists in this race will have the opportunity to wear the yellow jersey.

D    The cyclists travel by train and plane.

Common Core Standard RI.5.2; Common Core Standard RL.5.2

☐ **What is the best summary of this passage?**

A    The two rest days during the race allow the cyclists to recover from the vigorous pace of the race.

B    Only the leaders and the winner are allowed to wear the yellow jersey.

C    The most important bicycle race for most cyclists, the Tour de France, is held in Europe during July.

D    As the days progress, many cyclists drop out of the race.

Common Core Standard RI.5.2; Common Core Standard RL.5.2

☐ **Which is the best summary of the second paragraph?**

A    The race is physically demanding.

B    The winner does a victory lap during the race.

C    The route of the race can cause many cyclists problems.

D    The cyclists travel through several countries during the 23 day race.

**Common Core Standard RI.5.5**

☐ A cyclist gets to wear the yellow jersey because _____

A    he is predicted to win the race

B    he needs to be seen while cycling at night

C    he is proud

D    he is in the lead in the race

**Common Core Standard RI.5.5**

☐ A cyclist wears the white polka dot jersey because _____

A    he is in the lead

B    he is the best at climbing hills

C    he is the winner of the race

D    he is on a certain team

**Common Core Standard RI.5.5**

☐ The Tour de France takes 25 - 30 days to complete because _____

A    they must travel about 2,255 miles

B    the cyclists want to see the scenery

C    the prize money is $300,000

D    this race is the most impressive of all the bicycle races

Name _____

**Common Core Standard RI.5.8**

☐    The reason two alternative methods of transportation are used is so _____

    **A**    the cyclists don't get frustrated

    **B**    the cyclists can complete the course

    **C**    the cyclists can relax

    **D**    the cyclists can all be together

**Common Core Standard RI.5.8**

☐    The winner probably does a victory lap at a well-known location so that _____

    **A**    many people can watch

    **B**    they can charge admission

    **C**    the cyclist will know he has reached the end

    **D**    others will be able to bicycle with him

**Common Core Standard RI.5.8**

☐    We can predict that after the cyclists have been through a long hilly part of the course they will _____

    **A**    get lost

    **B**    approach the steep hills

    **C**    be tired

    **D**    give up

Common Core Standard RI.5.9

☐ Why is the yellow jersey more desirable than the other jerseys?

A    It is a prettier color than the other colors.

B    It can be seen from long distances.

C    The leader and winner wear the yellow jersey.

D    The sprinter cannot ride as fast as the climber.

Common Core Standard RI.5.9

☐ Why is this an important bicycle race for cyclists?  Use details from the passage to support your response.

_____

_____

_____

_____

_____

Common Core Standard RI.5.9

☐ Why do the cyclists in this race need two rest days?

A    They want to go sight-seeing.

B    They go through cities, farmlands, villages, and mountain ranges.

C    There are too many cyclists.

D    The race is about 2,255 miles long and takes 25 days.

**Common Core Standard RI.5.9**

☐     **You can tell from this passage that the Tour de France probably _____**

    **A**     **is expensive to watch**

    **B**     **is fun for the townspeople to enter**

    **C**     **draws many spectators**

    **D**     **has a $10 entry fee**

---

**Common Core Standard RI.5.9**

☐     **Which of these statements is best supported by information in the passage?**

    **A**     **The cyclists buy expensive bicycles.**

    **B**     **The cyclists must be experienced and in good health.**

    **C**     **The winner will spend the prize money in the United States.**

    **D**     **The spectators like bicycling.**

---

**Common Core Standard RI.5.9**

☐     **Information in the passage suggests that _____**

    **A**     **the cyclists in this race are among the best in the world**

    **B**     **this race is an easy victory for any cyclist**

    **C**     **the cyclists have been practicing for one year**

    **D**     **the yellow jersey is made out of cotton**

**Common Core Standard RL.5.3**

☐  The winner of the Tour de France probably feels _____

A    thoughtful

B    awkward

C    disoriented

D    thrilled

**Common Core Standard RL.5.3**

☐  The person who wears the yellow jersey probably feels _____

A    furious

B    depressed

C    excited

D    weightless

**Common Core Standard RL.5.3**

☐  How do the cyclists probably feel at the end of the day?

A    Exhausted

B    Funny

C    Puzzled

D    Angry

Name _____

Common Core Standard RI.5.3

[ ]   The Tour de France begins in France and ends in _____

A     Switzerland

B     Germany

C     the United States

D     France

Common Core Standard RI.5.3

[ ]   What could happen to a cyclist if their team members were not helpful during the race?

A     Learn to speak another language

B     Need to wear the yellow jersey

C     Not get enough food and drink

D      Win the race

Common Core Standard RI.5.3

[ ]   The route of the race could cause problems for the cyclists because _____

A     the race goes through many difficult kinds of terrain

B     the bicycles are expensive

C     the winners wear the yellow jersey

D     the winner must do a victory lap

Name _____

Common Core Standard RI.5.7

☐    **According to the map, most of the Tour de France takes place in _____**

A      Switzerland

B      Germany

C      United States

D      France

Common Core Standard RI.5.7

☐    **What country's border is near stage 10 and 11 on the map?**

A      Revel

B      Spain

C      Lourdes-Hautacam

D      Italy

Common Core Standard RI.5.7

☐    **According to the map, what will be the next city on the race after it leaves Lausanne?**

A      Fribourg-En-Brisgau

B      Mulhouse

C      Evian Les Bains

D      Belfort

**Common Core Standard RI.5.9**

☐     **The Champs-Elysees is located in** _____

     **A**     Switzerland

     **B**     Paris, France

     **C**     Houston, Texas

     **D**     Germany

---

**Common Core Standard RI.5.9**

☐     **Which city in Germany does the race go through?**

     **A**     Bern

     **B**     Mulhouse

     **C**     Fribourg-En-Brisgau

     **D**     Trier

---

**Common Core Standard RI.5.9**

☐     **Why do the cyclists need a rest day on July 12?**

     **A**     The plane ride was very tiring.

     **B**     They left Spain on stage 10.

     **C**     Avignon is a nice city to visit.

     **D**     They are entering a challenging part of the race.

Common Core Standard RI.5.6; Common Core Standard RL.5.6

☐ **Which of the following is a FACT from the passage?**

A    The race takes 25 to 30 days.

B    The race takes many months.

C    The winner of the Tour wears a green jersey.

D    To watch the Tour de France will only cost $10 per person.

---

Common Core Standard RI.5.6; Common Core Standard RL.5.6

☐ **Which of the following is an OPINION from the passage?**

A    The winner receives about $300,000.

B    The Tour de France is a prestigious race.

C    There are two days of rest during the race.

D    Cyclists love the beautiful scenery along the race route.

---

Common Core Standard RI.5.6; Common Core Standard RL.5.6

☐ **Which of the following is NOT an OPINION from the passage?**

A    This race goes through many beautiful cities.

B    This is a physically demanding race.

C    The leader at each stage gets to wear the yellow jersey.

D    This is a race for the best cyclists.

Name _____

Common Core Standard RL.5.8

☐ **A reader would probably read this passage to ____**

    **A**    **learn about foreign countries**

    **B**    **learn about the Tour de France**

    **C**    **learn how to draw maps**

    **D**    **learn how to ride a bicycle**

Common Core Standard RL.5.8

☐ **The purpose of this passage is to ____**

    **A**    **entertain the reader**

    **B**    **scare the reader**

    **C**    **inform the reader**

    **D**    **get people to like bicycles**

Common Core Standard RL.5.7

☐ **The author included a map of the race so ____**

    **A**    **the reader could follow the race on the map**

    **B**    **the reader could collect maps**

    **C**    **the reader could draw a map**

    **D**    **the reader could finish the map**

Common Core Standard RI.5.8; Common Core Standard RL.5.6

☐  **The author of the passage probably _____**

    **A**    knows many facts about the Tour de France

    **B**    dislikes cyclists

    **C**    does not know anything about bicycles

    **D**    likes to draw maps

---

Common Core Standard RI.5.8; Common Core Standard RL.5.6

☐  **The author of this passage probably believes _____**

    **A**    the cyclists are not in good physical shape

    **B**    this is an important race

    **C**    the map is too hard to read

    **D**    the yellow jersey is pretty

---

Common Core Standard RI.5.8; Common Core Standard RL.5.6

☐  **You can tell from the passage that the author _____**

    **A**    won the race

    **B**    owns a racing bicycle

    **C**    has been to France

    **D**    is interested in the Tour de France

# ANSWER KEY

### WHAT IS CELEBRATED ON DIA DE LOS MUERTOS?

| | |
|---|---|
| Page 2 | C, A, B |
| Page 3 | D, B, A |
| Page 4 | D, B, C |
| Page 5 | B, D, C |
| Page 6 | C, D, Open |
| Page 7 | B, C, A |
| Page 8 | D, Open, Open |
| Page 9 | C, A, D |
| Page 10 | D, B, C |
| Page 11 | B, C, A |
| Page 12 | A, C, D |
| Page 13 | C, D, B |
| Page 14 | B, C, D |
| Page 15 | A, D, B |
| Page 16 | C, A, D |
| Page 17 | A, D, C |
| Page 18 | C, D, B |
| Page 19 | Open |

### WHO WILL WIN THE ESSAY CONTEST?

| | |
|---|---|
| Page 22 | B, A, C |
| Page 23 | C, D, B |
| Page 24 | C, B, D |
| Page 25 | B, C, A |
| Page 26 | D |
| Page 27 | C, B, D |
| Page 28 | D, B, Open |
| Page 29 | D, Open, B |
| Page 30 | B, Open, D |
| Page 31 | C, D, B |
| Page 32 | C, A, B |
| Page 33 | B, D, A |
| Page 34 | Open, C, Open |
| Page 35 | B, C, A |
| Page 36 | D, B, C |
| Page 37 | B, D, A |
| Page 38 | C, B, A |
| Page 39 | Open |

### THE ELECTION

| | |
|---|---|
| Page 41 | D, C, B |
| Page 42 | B, D, A |
| Page 43 | D, B, C |
| Page 44 | B, D, C |
| Page 45 | C, B, D |
| Page 46 | B, Open, A |
| Page 47 | C, D, B |
| Page 48 | B, D, C |
| Page 49 | B, C, D |
| Page 50 | B, D, C |

| | |
|---|---|
| Page 51 | C, A, B |
| Page 52 | D, B, C |
| Page 53 | B, A, C |
| Page 54 | D, A, B |
| Page 55 | C, B, D |
| Page 56 | C, D, B |
| Page 57 | B, C, D |
| Page 58 | B, D, A |
| Page 59 | C, B, A |
| Page 60 | A, C, A |
| Page 61 | Open |

### MANATEES: GENTLE GIANTS

| | |
|---|---|
| Page 65 | B, A, C |
| Page 66 | C, B, A |
| Page 67 | D, C, B |
| Page 68 | B |
| Page 69 | B, D, C |
| Page 70 | B, D, A |
| Page 71 | D, A, C |
| Page 72 | B, D, C |
| Page 73 | C, B, D |
| Page 74 | C, B, D |
| Page 75 | B, D, A |
| Page 76 | D, A, B |
| Page 77 | C, B, A |
| Page 78 | D, B, C |
| Page 79 | B, D, C |

### THE TOUR DE FRANCE

| | |
|---|---|
| Page 81 | C, B, A |
| Page 82 | A, C, D |
| Page 83 | B, D, C |
| Page 84 | B, A, C |
| Page 85 | C, B, Open |
| Page 86 | D, B, A |
| Page 87 | B, A, D |
| Page 88 | D, A, B |
| Page 89 | B, C, A |
| Page 90 | D, B, A |
| Page 91 | B, A, C |
| Page 92 | C, Open, D |
| Page 93 | C, B, A |
| Page 94 | D, C, A |
| Page 95 | D, C, A |
| Page 96 | D, B, A |
| Page 97 | B, C, D |
| Page 98 | A, B, C |
| Page 99 | B, C, A |
| Page 100 | A, B, D |

Made in United States
North Haven, CT
17 March 2023

34186080R00061